FINDING NEMO

Read Along

• Storybook •

Long tail Books

ISBN 979-11-91343-57-1 14740
Longtail Books

Disney · PIXAR
FINDING NEMO

Read Along

Storybook

Nemo was a little **clownfish** who lived a quiet life with his dad, Marlin, on the Great Barrier **Reef**. Nemo **long**ed **for adventure**, but Marlin worried about the **danger**s of the **ocean**. He **barely** let Nemo out of his **sight**.

On the first day of school, Marlin **overhear**d Nemo and his
new friends **daring** each other to swim out over a **steep cliff**.
"Come on, Nemo! How far can you go?"

Marlin **panic**ked. "Nemo, you know you can't swim well."

"I can swim fine, Dad. Okay?"

Nemo **dart**ed up **toward** a boat on the **surface**. His
father **yell**ed after him. "Get back here! I said, get back
here, now!"

As Nemo swam, a **diver appear**ed behind him.

The diver pulled out a **net** and caught Nemo. Then he **return**ed to his boat and **sped** off, **accidentally knock**ing one of his **mask**s **overboard**.

Marlin **chase**d after the boat, but it was too fast. "Nemo! Nemo, no! NO!" Marlin **search**ed everywhere. "Has anybody seen a boat? Please?"

Marlin soon **bump**ed **into** a **blue tang** fish named Dory who **offer**ed to help.

"Hey, I've seen a boat! And it went this way! Follow me!" When Marlin followed, Dory **whirl**ed around. "Stop following me, okay?"

"What are you talking about? You're showing me which way the boat went."

Dory looked **surprised**, then shook her head sadly. "I'm so sorry. See, I- I **suffer** from **short**-**term memory loss**."

Figuring Dory couldn't help him, Marlin turned to leave and found himself **face-to-face** with a shark!

The shark **invite**d Dory and Marlin to a "**get-together**" in an old **sunken** ship.

Dory was excited. "You mean like a party?"

Inside the ship were two other sharks, and together they **pledge**d: "I am a nice shark, not a **mindless** eating machine. Fish are friends, not food."

As they spoke, Marlin looked up and saw the diver's mask! Dory **notice**d some writing on the **strap**. It might be a **clue** to help them find Nemo! Marlin and Dory quickly left the "party," carrying the mask.

Miles away, Nemo had been taken to a fish **tank** in a **dentist**'s office. A **goofy gang** of **tropical fish** lived there. The fish and their friend Nigel, a **pelican**, **pass**ed the time by watching the dentist work.

That night, Nemo learned that he would be given to Darla, the dentist's **niece**. The Tank Gang **warn**ed him that Darla's fish never lived for very long. Nemo's new friends didn't want anything bad to happen to him.

Their leader, Gill, **took charge**. "We're going to help him **escape**."

Gill explained that if someone could **jam** the water **filter,** the dentist would take the fish out of the tank to clean it. When he put the fish in plastic bags, they could escape by **roll**ing out the window and into the **harbor**.

But who would be **brave** enough to **break** the **dangerous** filter?

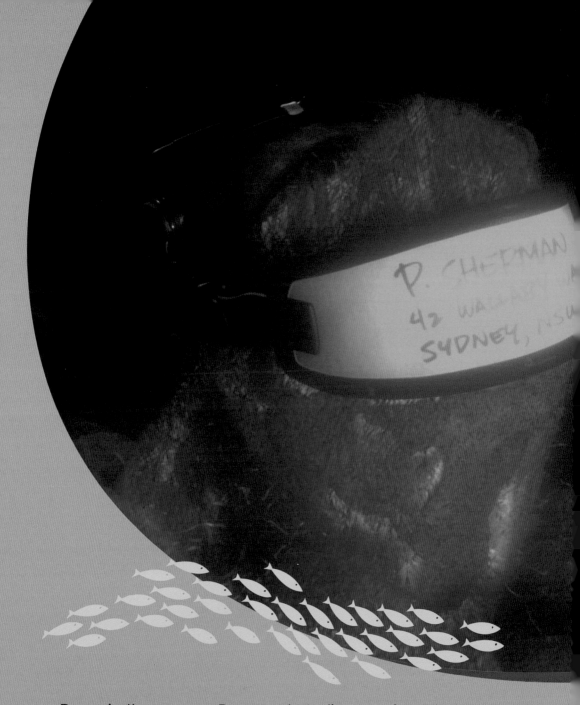

Deep in the ocean, Dory and Marlin were in a dark **canyon**. Marlin **struggle**d to **hold on to** the lighted **antenna** of a dangerous **anglerfish** so that Dory could read what was written on the mask. "P. Sherman, 42 Wallaby Way, Sydney."

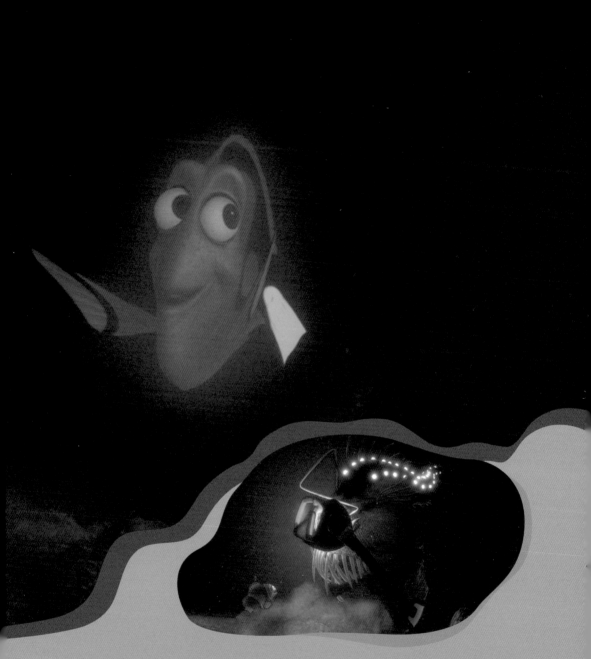

All of a sudden, the anglerfish got **loose**. "**Duck**!" The **giant** fish **crash**ed above them, **wedging** himself between the mask and a rock. Marlin breathed a **sigh** of **relief**. This was **turn**ing **out** to be quite an adventure!

Marlin and Dory **head**ed for Sydney. Suddenly, Dory bumped into a **teeny-tiny jellyfish**. "I shall call him Squishy, and he shall be mine."

But Squishy wasn't **alone**. Soon, they were **surround**ed by an **entire forest** of **deadly** jellyfish. The jellyfish **stung** Dory and Marlin, too, making them feel **weak** and tired.

As the ocean **fade**d around him, the last thing Marlin saw was the **shadow** of a giant **sea turtle**.

When Marlin woke
up, he was lying on the sea turtle's **shell**.
The turtle **introduce**d himself. "Dude! Name's Crush."

Around them, hundreds of sea turtles **rode** with a **lightning-fast
current**. Marlin told Crush and his son Squirt the story of his search
for Nemo. "I live on this reef a long, long way from here. . . ."

Dory had already **forgotten** the story. "This is going to be good. I can tell!"

Squirt told the story to a lobster, the lobster told a dolphin, and soon the news **spread all the way** to Sydney, where Nigel the pelican heard it.

Nigel sped off to the dentist's office to tell Nemo. "Your dad's been fighting the entire ocean **look**ing **for** you. And the word is, he's headed this way right now—to Sydney!"

"Really?" Nemo couldn't believe his dad was so **adventurous**! Marlin was **risk**ing everything to **save** him. Nemo **realize**d that if he was ever going to get home, he had to be brave, too.

He took a deep breath and **carefully jam**med a **pebble** into the tank's filter, stopping its **swirl**ing **blade**s. Soon, the tank would be so dirty the dentist would *have* to clean it. . . .

But in the morning, the tank was still clean! The filter had
been changed during the night, **ruin**ing their escape **plan**.
Then, the dentist **slip**ped a net into the water, **capturing** Nemo.

"Help me!"

Thinking fast, Gill **charge**d into the net and shouted to Nemo.
"Swim down!" He did, pulling down the net and escaping—
straight into a **plastic bag** the dentist was holding.

The dentist started to **hand** Darla the bag, but then he saw Nemo inside, **belly** up. Nemo **wink**ed at his friends. He was only **pretend**ing to be dead. The gang **cheer**ed. "He's going to get **flush**ed down the **toilet**. He's going to **get out of** here!"

Outside Sydney, Marlin and Dory had met Nigel, who flew them straight to the dentist's office. The pelican **soar**ed inside with the two fish in his **beak**.

Marlin saw Nemo **float**ing **upside down** in the bag. "Nemo!" Marlin thought his son was dead. The dentist **shoo**ed Nigel away. "Out with ya. And stay out!"

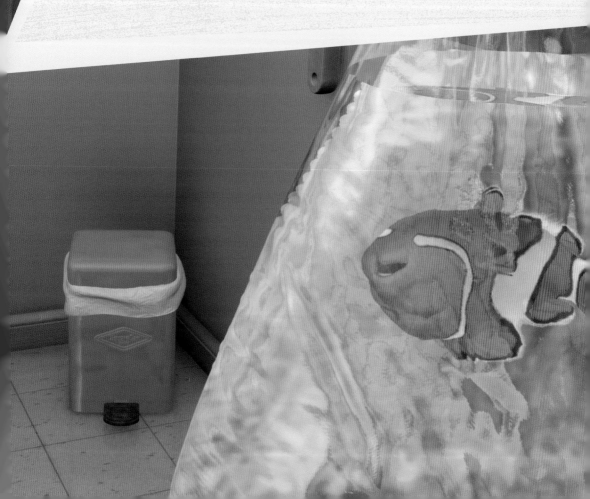

Nigel returned to the harbor. He **drop**ped Marlin and Dory into the water. Marlin swam out to sea, leaving Dory. "We were too late. I'm going home now."

After Marlin left, Nemo swam out of a **nearby pipe**. He had been flushed! Nemo **spot**ted Dory swimming in **circle**s. "Are you all right? I'm Nemo."

"Ahh! You're Nemo!" Dory **hug**ged him happily.

Nemo and Dory searched for Marlin, spotting him in the nearby **fishing ground**s.

"Daddy!"

"Nemo! I'm coming, Nemo!"

As they swam toward each other, a big net dropped into the water and captured lots of fish, **including** Dory! But Nemo knew **exactly** what to do. "Tell all the fish to swim down!"

Nemo even swam inside the net to help.
Together, the fish swam down until the net
broke. Everyone was free!

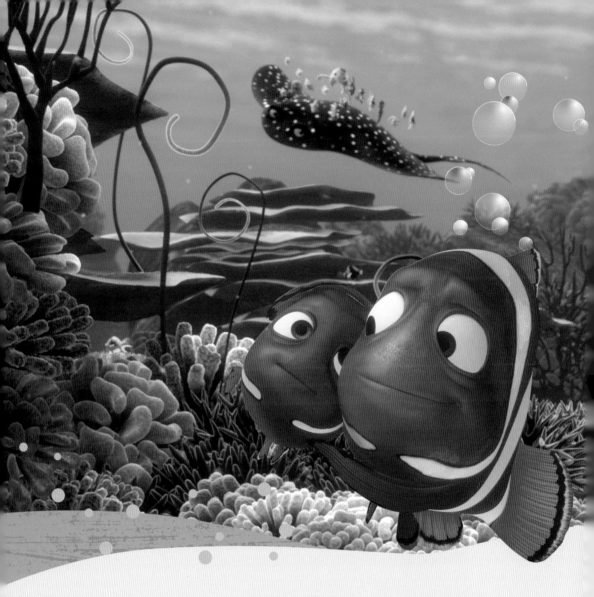

Several weeks later, Nemo was back home and ready for school. This time, Marlin was ready, too. He knew that his son could **take care of** himself.

Nemo **wave**d as he swam away. "Bye, Dad. Oh, wait! I forgot something!" He swam back and hugged Marlin. "Love you, Dad."

Marlin smiled. "I love you, too, son. Now, go have an adventure!"

Read-Along

Dive into an ocean of
adventure!

This is the story of Nemo's amazing

underwater adventure. Meet Nemo, Marlin,

Dory, and all your favorite Finding Nemo

characters in this exciting storybook.

Disney · PIXAR

FINDING
NEMO

Read
Along

Read Along

워크북

이 책은 메인북인 **워크북**과 별책인 **스토리북**, 전 2권으로 분리하여 볼 수 있습니다. 스토리북을 통해 영화의 내용을 영어로 가볍게 읽고 워크북으로 알차게 학습해 보세요.

워크북의 구성

스토리북을 네 개의 파트로 나누어 다양한 액티비티를 담았습니다. 워크북에 담긴 즐거운 활동을 통해 영어 실력을 키워 보세요!

Fun Fact

각 파트마다 영화 내용과 관련된 흥미로운 이야기를 수록하여, 스토리북을 보다 알차게 읽을 수 있도록 구성했습니다. 다양한 주제로 쓰인 흥미로운 글을 통해 영어 읽기의 재미를 느껴 보세요.

Vocabulary

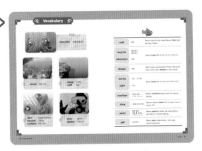

스토리북 본문에서 굵은 글씨로 표시된 주요 단어들을 각 파트별로 정리했습니다. 그림과 예문이 함께 나와 있어 단어의 뜻을 쉽게 이해할 수 있습니다.

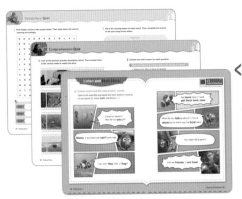

Learning Activities

다채로운 학습 액티비티로 나만의 영어 실력을 쌓아 보세요. 단어, 표현, 그리고 내용 이해까지 확실하게 짚어 줍니다.

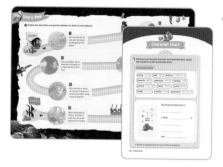

Review

워크북에 수록된 스티커를 이용하여 이야기 지도와 좋아하는 캐릭터에 대한 소개까지 완성해 보세요. 자연스럽게 이야기를 다시 확인하고 정리할 수 있습니다.

Translation

스토리북의 내용이 완전히 이해되지 않는다면, 워크북 속 친절한 한국어 번역을 확인해 보세요. 최대한 직역에 가깝게 번역되어 원서 읽기의 길잡이가 되어 줍니다.

오디오북

듣기 훈련용   따라 읽기용

QR코드를 인식하여 '듣기 훈련용 오디오북'과 '따라 읽기용 오디오북'의 두 가지 오디오북을 들어 보세요! '듣기 훈련용 오디오북'은 영화 속 캐릭터 목소리와 재미있는 효과음이 곁들여진 오리지널 오디오북입니다. 원서의 내용을 실감나게 듣고 즐길 수 있습니다. '따라 읽기용 오디오북'은 조금 더 천천히 정확한 발음으로 녹음한 오디오북입니다. 학습용으로 다양하게 활용할 수 있습니다.

---

2 ## 스토리북의 구성

별책으로 분리하여 더욱 가볍게 읽을 수 있는 스토리북! 간결한 이야기와 함께 영화 속 장면과 대사가 담겨 있어 영화의 재미와 감동을 다시 한 번 느낄 수 있습니다. 이야기에 나오는 주요 단어를 굵은 글씨로 강조하여, 문맥 속의 단어들을 더 확실히 인지하도록 도와줍니다.

Contents

· Part ·

1

스토리북 p.2~9

Working together

A sea anemone is a creature that attaches itself to a rock and has long, arm-like tentacles that can sting fish. Clownfish can live with the anemone without getting hurt because it has a slimy layer that keeps it safe from the stings.

The anemone and clownfish help each other. The anemone provides protection for the clownfish, and the clownfish attracts food to the anemone and helps to clean it.

Vocabulary

clownfish [동물] 흰동가리

ocean 대양, 바다

steep 가파른
cliff 절벽

dart 쏜살같이 움직이다
toward ~쪽으로
surface 수면, 표면

diver 잠수부
appear 나타나다

reef	암초	Nemo lived on the Great Barrier **Reef** with his dad, Marlin.
long for	열망하다, 갈망하다	
		Nemo **long**ed **for** a life full of adventure.
adventure	모험	
danger	위험	Marlin was worried about Nemo because there were many **danger**s in the ocean.
barely	거의 ~ 아니게	
		Marlin **barely** let his son out of his sight.
sight	시야	
overhear	우연히 듣다 (과거형 overheard)	Marlin **overhear**d Nemo and his friends talking.
dare	~를 해 보라고 하다	Nemo's friends **dare**d him to swim over a steep cliff.
panic	겁에 질려 어쩔 줄 모르다 (과거형 panicked)	Marlin **panic**ked when he heard Nemo and Nemo's friends talking.
yell	소리치다	Marlin **yell**ed after Nemo, who was swimming away.

Vocabulary

net 그물

speed 빨리 가다
(과거형 sped)

mask 수중 마스크
overboard 배 밖으로

search 찾아보다, 수색하다

bump into ~와 마주치다
blue tang [동물] 블루탱

face-to-face 마주보는

return	돌아가다	The diver **return**ed to his boat with Nemo in his net.
accidentally	뜻하지 않게	The diver **accidentally** knocked one of his masks into the water.
knock	쳐서 움직이게 하다	
chase	뒤쫓다	Marlin **chase**d the boat and looked everywhere for Nemo.
offer	제안하다	Dory **offer**ed to help Marlin find the boat.
whirl	빙빙 돌다	Dory **whirl**ed around and told Marlin to stop following her.
surprised	놀란	Dory was **surprised** when Marlin said that she was helping him.
suffer	(병을) 앓다	
short-term memory	단기 기억	Dory **suffer**ed from short-term memory loss.
loss	상실	
figure	판단하다	Marlin **figure**d that Dory could not help him find the boat.

Vocabulary Quiz

1 Find hidden words in the puzzle below. Then write down the correct meaning accordingly.

O	H	A	D	R	K	A	I	D	L	K	L
B	W	L	M	R	S	D	J	Y	I	N	Z
A	D	V	E	N	T	U	R	E	V	O	M
R	Y	S	D	T	G	U	I	O	S	C	V
E	X	T	Z	G	D	R	H	I	O	K	I
L	P	D	A	N	G	E	R	G	F	H	S
Y	Z	N	E	M	O	T	S	F	G	W	I
S	D	O	R	Y	I	U	H	A	R	B	G
C	R	F	I	G	U	R	E	R	E	A	H
Q	D	H	T	D	T	N	K	Y	E	F	T
K	I	T	A	P	D	L	N	G	F	R	M
F	C	H	A	S	E	Y	D	I	Z	X	Z

reef	암초	adventure		danger	
barely		sight		return	
knock		chase		figure	

2 **Fill in the missing letters for each word. Then complete the answer to the quiz using those letters.**

① __S__urface 수면, 표면

② st__ep 가파른

③ d__ __t 쏜살같이 움직이다 *two letters

④ __lownfis__ [동물] 흰동가리 *two letters

⑤ div__r 잠수부

⑥ towar__ ~쪽으로

⑦ blue t__ng [동물] 블루탱

⑧ __earch 찾아보다, 수색하다

⑨ mas__ 수중 마스크

⑩ ov__rboar__ 배 밖으로 *two letters

⑪ __ump int__ ~와 마주치다 *two letters

⑫ __ppear 나타나다

⑬ face-__o-face 마주보는

QUIZ

What did Marlin do after he chased after the boat?

ANSWER

He __S__ _ _ _ _ _ _ _ everywhere and _ _ _ _ _ _

if anybody had seen a _ _ _ _ .

Comprehension Quiz

1 Look at the pictures and the description below. Then number them in the correct order to match the story.

A diver caught Nemo and took him back on his boat.

Marlin was worried about Nemo, so he barely let Nemo out of his sight.

1

Marlin met Dory and asked for her help in finding the boat.

Marlin chased the boat, but he was not fast enough to catch it.

2 Choose the best answer for each question.

1 What were Nemo's new friends doing on the first day of school?

a) Daring each other to follow the teacher

b) Trying to get each other to swim over a steep cliff

c) Racing to see who was the fastest swimmer

2 What did Dory do when she noticed that Marlin was following her?

a) She told him to swim faster.

b) She told him to stop following her.

c) She asked him to help find the boat.

3 Why did Marlin decide to leave Dory?

a) He was angry that she did not want to look for Nemo.

b) He was afraid that she was friends with a shark.

c) He thought she could not help him find the boat.

3 Read each sentence and decide whether it is true or false.

1 Nemo was afraid of the dangers of the ocean.	true	false
2 Marlin thought that Nemo could not swim very well.	true	false
3 The diver caught Nemo with his hands.	true	false
4 The diver threw his mask into the water on purpose.	true	false
5 Dory had a problem with remembering things.	true	false

· Part ·
2

스토리북 p.10~17

A colorful fish

The blue tang fish is not always blue! Young blue tang fish are actually bright yellow.

As adults, blue tang fish may change their color based on what is going on around them. For example, when they are feeling stressed, they change to a dark purple color.

Vocabulary

get-together 모임

strap 스트랩, 끈

tank 수조

gang 무리, 패거리
tropical fish [동물] 열대어

pelican [동물] 펠리컨

niece 조카딸

invite	초대하다	The shark **invite**d Dory and Marlin to go inside a sunken ship.
sunken	침몰한	
pledge	맹세하다	The sharks **pledge**d that they would be nice and not eat the fish.
mindless	아무 생각이 없는	The sharks did not want to be **mindless** and eat everything they saw.
notice	알아차리다	Dory **notice**d some writing on the diver's mask.
clue	단서	The driver's mask might give Marlin a **clue**.
dentist	치과 의사	The **dentist** had a tank in his office, where Nemo was sent.
goofy	별난, 바보 같은	Nemo met a **goofy** group of fish in the fish tank at the dentist's office.
pass	(시간을) 보내다	The fish **pass**ed the time by watching the dentist as he worked.
warn	경고하다	The fish in the Tang Gang **warn**ed Nemo that Darla was dangerous.
take charge	지휘를 맡다, 책임지다	Gill **took charge** and decided they should help Nemo get back to the ocean.
escape	탈출하다	The fish planned to help Nemo **escape** from the tank.
jam	고장나게 하다*, 밀어 넣다	Gill said that someone needed to **jam** the water filter to escape.

✳ Vocabulary ✳

filter   필터, 여과 장치

harbor   항구

canyon   협곡

struggle   애쓰다, 노력하다

antenna   촉각, 더듬이
anglerfish   [동물] 아귀

giant   거대한
wedge   끼워 넣다

roll	구르다	After the fish were put in bags, they would **roll** out the window to escape.
brave	용감한	One of the fish needed to be **brave** to make the plan work.
break	깨다, 부수다	It would not be easy to **break** the dangerous filter.
dangerous	위험한	
hold on to	~을 계속 잡고 있다	Marlin **held on to** the light from the anglerfish so that Dory could look at the mask.
all of a sudden	갑자기	**All of a sudden**, the anglerfish that Marlin was holding got loose.
loose	풀린, 묶여 있지 않은	
duck	피하다	Marlin told Dory to **duck** as the giant anglerfish came toward them.
crash	부딪치다	The anglerfish **crash**ed above Marlin and Dory.
sigh	한숨	Marlin let out a **sigh** of relief because the anglerfish got stuck.
relief	안도	
turn out	되다	Marlin's search for Nemo was **turning out** to be a big adventure.

Vocabulary Quiz

1 Use the clues below to fill in the crossword puzzle.

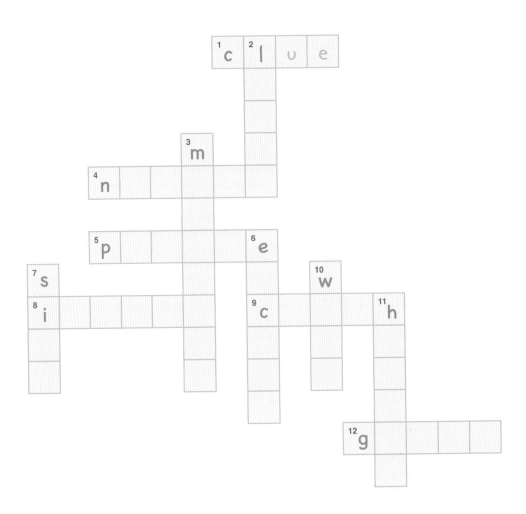

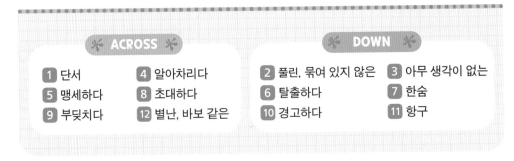

2 Fill in the missing letters for each word. Then complete the answer to the quiz using those letters.

① __edge 끼워 넣다

② __ntenna 촉각, 더듬이

③ __iece 조카딸

④ __ank 수조

⑤ pelic__ __ [동물] 펠리컨 *two letters

⑥ can__on 협곡

⑦ get-__oget__er 모임 *two letters

⑧ f__lter 필터, 여과 장치

⑨ ga__g 무리, 패거리

⑩ stru__gle 애쓰다, 노력하다

⑪ anglerfis__ [동물] 아귀

⑫ str__ __ 스트랩, 끈 *two letters

⑬ tro__ical fish [동물] 열대어

⑭ d__ __tist 치과 의사 *two letters

QUIZ

Why did Nemo's new friends want to help him escape?

ANSWER

They did not __ __ __ __ __   __ __ __ __ __ __ __ __

bad to __ __ __ __ __ __ to him.

Comprehension Quiz

1 Choose the sentence which best describes the picture to match the story.

A Gill explained his plan to make the fish tank clean.

B The Tank Gang wanted Nemo to try to bite the dentist.

C Nemo found out that the dentist would give him to Darla.

A Dory tried to read what was written on the mask.

B Dory struggled to pull the mask off the rock.

C Dory wanted to leave a message for Nemo on the mask.

2 Choose the best answer for each question.

1 What did the fish in the tank do to pass the time?

a) They played games in the water.

b) They asked Nigel the pelican to bring them things.

c) They watched the dentist working in his office.

2 What did the Tank Gang imply about Darla?

a) That she visited the dentist's office every day

b) That she did not care for her fish well

c) That she liked to clean the tank

3 Why were Marlin and Dory interested in the mask?

a) They thought it might be a clue for finding Nemo.

b) They thought it might help them travel faster.

c) They thought it would protect them from dangerous fish.

3 Read each sentence and decide whether it is true or false.

❶ Dory was excited to go to the sunken ship with the shark.	true	false
❷ The shark took Marlin and Dory to the sunken ship because he wanted to eat them.	true	false
❸ Nemo came up with a plan to escape from the tank.	true	false
❹ Marlin thought it was easy to hold on to the antenna of the anglerfish.	true	false
❺ Marlin was relieved when the anglerfish got stuck between the mask and a rock.	true	false

Listen and Read Along

🔊 **Listen and read the characters' words.**

Listen to the audio files and repeat after each sentence, focusing on your pause (**/**), stress (**bold**), and linking (⌢).

Come on, Nemo! /
How far can **you** go?

Nemo, / you know you **can't** swim well.

I can swim **fine**, Dad. / O**kay**?

• Part •
3

스토리북 p.18~23

Noisy jaws

Clownfish can communicate by hitting the jaws of their mouth together, which creates a knocking sound.

They can use the sound to warn other clownfish to stay away from their home. They will attack if the warning is not followed.

Scientists discovered this unusual way of communicating by using X-ray and video technology.

Vocabulary

teeny-tiny   조그마한
jellyfish   [동물] 해파리

surround   둘러싸다
forest   숲을 이룬 것

sting   쏘다
(과거형 stung)

weak   힘이 없는

head	가다, 향하다	Marlin **head**ed for Sydney, Australia, with Dory.
alone	혼자	The tiny jellyfish, Squishy, was not **alone**.
entire **deadly**	전체의 치명적인	Marlin and Dory were in the middle of an **entire** forest of deadly jellyfish.
fade	점점 희미해지다	The ocean seemed to **fade** around Marlin and Dory after they got stung by the jellyfish.
introduce	소개하다	Crush **introduce**d himself when Marlin woke up.
ride (과거형 rode) **lightning-fast** **current**	타다 번개 같이 빠른 해류	Marlin saw the sea turtles **ride**ing with a lightning-fast current.

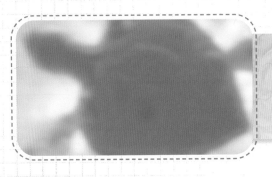

shadow   그림자

sea turtle   [동물] 바다거북
shell   등딱지

pebble   조약돌

swirl   빙빙 돌다
blade   (엔진의) 날개깃

forget	잊다 (과거분사형 forgotten)	Dory had **forgotten** the story about Marlin's search for Nemo.
spread all the way	퍼지다 (과거형 spread) 멀리	Marlin's story **spread** all the way to Sydney, where Nigel heard it.
look for	~을 찾다	Nigel told Nemo that his dad was **looking** for him.
adventurous	모험심이 강한, 대담한	Nemo was surprised that his dad was being so **adventurous**.
risk save	~의 위험을 무릅쓰다 구하다	Marlin was **risk**ing everything to find and save Nemo.
realize	깨닫다	Nemo **realize**d that he had to be brave so that he could get home.
carefully	신중하게, 조심스럽게	Nemo **carefully** put a pebble in the filter to break it.
jam	밀어 넣다*, 고장나게 하다	Nemo **jam**med a pebble into the tank's filter and its swirling blades stopped.

Vocabulary Quiz

1 Find hidden words in the puzzle below. Then write down the correct meaning accordingly.

M	Q	F	B	P	X	E	A	F	E	P	A
A	U	O	I	D	I	I	F	L	O	W	L
C	U	R	R	E	N	T	E	R	Y	P	O
M	R	G	A	E	T	L	G	I	L	F	N
C	Y	E	B	A	R	A	K	F	A	D	E
O	A	T	O	Z	O	L	S	H	A	R	K
D	T	K	L	M	D	A	I	U	D	S	B
E	L	E	A	P	U	L	E	F	K	P	D
A	V	A	T	O	C	A	L	Q	J	R	H
D	Q	Z	K	L	E	N	T	I	R	E	T
L	B	I	H	E	Q	N	A	E	I	A	S
Y	K	E	S	H	A	D	O	W	N	D	E

alone		entire		deadly	
fade		shadow		introduce	
current		forget		spread	

2 Fill in the missing letters for each word. Then complete the answer to the quiz using those letters.

① p__bble 조약돌

② surrou__d 둘러싸다

③ sea __urtle [동물] 바다거북

④ sw___ __l 빙빙 돌다 *two letters

⑤ blad___ (엔진의) 날개깃

⑥ shel___ 등딱지

⑦ f__rest 숲을 이룬 것

⑧ shad__w 그림자

⑨ wea___ 힘이 없는

⑩ st__ __ __ 쏘다 *three letters

⑪ jellyfis___ [동물] 해파리

⑫ teeny-t__ny 조그마한

⑬ ja___ 밀어 넣다, 고장나게 하다

QUIZ

What did Nigel the pelican tell Nemo?

ANSWER

The pelican told him that Marlin was searching the __ __ __ __ __ __

ocean __ __ __ __ __ for __ __ .

Comprehension Quiz

1 Look at the pictures and the description below. Then number them in the correct order to match the story.

Dory and Marlin got stung by some jellyfish.

Nigel told Nemo that his dad was looking for him.

The news of Marlin's search for Nemo spread across the ocean.

Crush brought Marlin and Dory to Sydney on his back.

2 Choose the best answer for each question.

1 What did Marlin see after the jellyfish stung him?

a) The shadow of a sunken ship
b) The shadow of a sea turtle
c) The shadow of the diver's mask

2 How did Marlin get to Sydney quickly?

a) He rode on a sea turtle's back.
b) He jumped onto a boat.
c) He followed some jellyfish.

3 What did Nemo put into the tank's filter?

a) A pebble
b) A blade
c) Some fish food

3 Read each sentence and decide whether it is true or false.

1 Squishy was all alone in the ocean.   true   false

2 Dory did not remember the story about Marlin's search for Nemo.   true   false

3 The sea animals told Marlin's story to each other until the news reached Nigel.   true   false

4 Nemo was surprised that his dad went on an adventure to find him.   true   false

5 Nemo decided that he should be brave so that he could escape.   true   false

• Part •
4

스토리북 p.24~32

A fierce fighter

The blue tang fish may look cute like Dory, but it is one tough fish. It has sharp spines sticking out of its tail.

When it is in danger, the blue tang fish will swing its tail from side to side to hit the predator. The spines also have a poison in them that can hurt the predator.

Vocabulary

slip   (슬며시) 넣다
capture   포획하다

charge   급히 가다

plastic bag   비닐봉지

belly   배, 복부
wink   윙크하다
pretend   ~인 척하다

ruin	망치다	The changed filter **ruin**ed the plan to escape.
plan	계획	

straight	곧장	Nemo swam **straight** into the plastic bag.

hand	건네주다	Nemo had his belly up when the dentist **hand**ed the bag to Darla.

cheer	환호하다	Nemo's friends **cheer**ed when they realized Nemo's new plan.

flush	(물을 쏟아) 씻어 없애다	Nemo's friends thought the dentist would **flush** Nemo down the toilet.
toilet	변기	

get out of	~에서 나오다, 도망치다	Nemo's friends were happy that Nemo would **get out of** the tank.

soar	날아오르다	Nigel **soar**ed inside the dentist's office with Marlin and Dory in his beak.

Vocabulary

beak　(새의) 부리

float　(물에) 뜨다
upside down　(아래위가) 거꾸로

hug　껴안다

wave　손을 흔들어 인사하다

shoo	훠이 하고 쫓아내다	The dentist **shoo**ed Nigel away from the window.
drop	떨어뜨리다	Nigel **drop**ped Marlin and Dory back into the water.
nearby	바로 가까이의	Nemo swam out of a **nearby** pipe and met Dory.
pipe	관, 파이프	
spot	발견하다	Nemo **spott**ed Dory, who was swimming around in circles.
circle	동그라미, 원	
fishing ground	어장	Nemo and Dory found Marlin at some **fishing ground**s.
include	포함하다	The fishing net captured a lot of fish, **including** Dory.
exactly	정확히	Nemo knew **exactly** what he should do to save Dory.
take care of	~을 돌보다	Marlin knew that Nemo could **take care of** himself.

Vocabulary Quiz

1 Use the clues below to fill in the crossword puzzle.

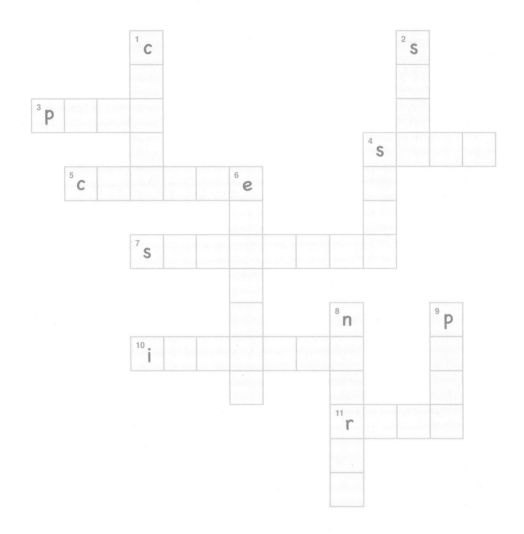

Crossword clues:

✳ ACROSS ✳

3 관, 파이프
4 날아오르다
5 동그라미, 원
7 곧장
10 포함하다
11 망치다

✳ DOWN ✳

1 환호하다
2 휘이 하고 쫓아내다
4 발견하다
6 정확히
8 바로 가까이의
9 계획

2 Fill in the missing letters for each word. Then complete the answer to the quiz using those letters.

1. ups___de dow___ (아래위가) 거꾸로 *two letters

2. ___l___p (슬며시) 넣다 *two letters

3. preten___ ~인 척하다

4. captur___ 포획하다

5. ___lush (물을 쏟아) 씻어 없애다

6. ___nclude 포함하다

7. pla___tic bag 비닐봉지

8. ___and 건네주다

9. ___elly 배, 복부

10. wav___ 손을 흔들어 인사하다

11. ch___rge 급히 가다

12. win___ 윙크하다

How did Nemo and Dory go to the dentist's office?

The pelican went ___ ___ ___ ___ ___ ___ with the two

___ ___ ___ in his ___ ___ ___ .

Comprehension Quiz

1 **Choose the sentence which best describes the picture to match the story.**

(A) Nigel brought Marlin and Dory to the wrong place.

(B) Marlin and Dory were surprised that Darla was so mean.

(C) Marlin was surprised because he saw Nemo in a plastic bag.

(A) Marlin took Nemo home instead of sending him to school.

(B) Marlin wanted to go on an adventure with Nemo.

(C) Marlin knew that Nemo was able to take care of himself.

2 Choose the best answer for each question.

1 Why was the tank still clean in the morning?

a) The dentist cleaned the tank with a net.

b) Nemo's pebble had fallen out during the night.

c) Someone had already changed the filter.

2 Why did Nemo wink at his friends?

a) To prove that he was still alive

b) To signal to them that he needed help quickly

c) To show that he thought the situation was funny

3 How did Nemo get into the ocean?

a) He jumped out of the window.

b) He was flushed down a toilet.

c) He got picked up by Nigel.

3 Read each sentence and decide whether it is true or false.

① Gill taught Nemo how to swim up to the top of the tank.	true	false
② Nigel was carrying Marlin and Dory in his beak.	true	false
③ Marlin found Nemo at the fishing grounds.	true	false
④ The fish got free from the net by swimming down together.	true	false
⑤ In the end, Marlin told Nemo to have adventures.	true	false

📢 **Listen and read the characters' words.**

Listen to the audio files and repeat after each sentence, focusing on your pause (**/**), stress (**bold**), and linking (⌒).

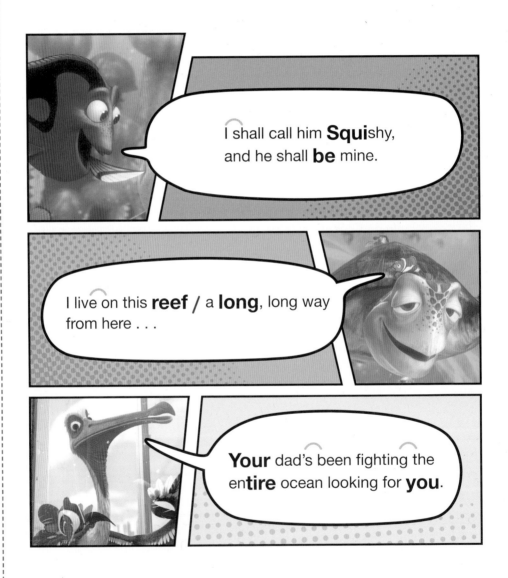

I shall call him **Squi**shy, and he shall **be** mine.

I live on this **reef** / a **long**, long way from here . . .

Your dad's been fighting the en**tire** ocean looking for **you**.

Story Map

⭐ Follow the story line and put the stickers on their correct places!

START

1

Nemo's dad, Marlin, was worried about the dangers of the ocean.

4

Dory and Marlin found the diver's address on a mask that fell off the boat.

5

Dory and Marlin woke up riding to Sydney on a turtle's back after being stung by jellyfish.

FINISH

8

Nemo went back to school, and Marlin knew his son could take care of himself.

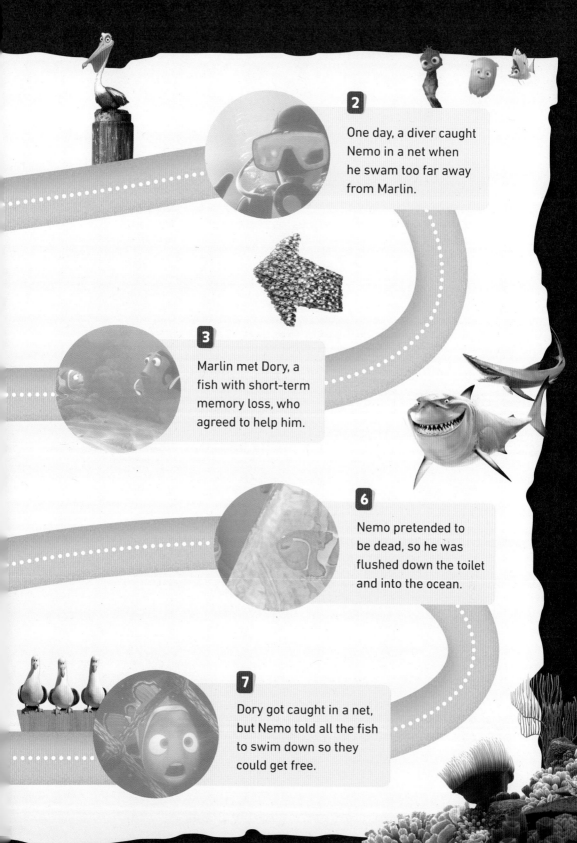

2

One day, a diver caught Nemo in a net when he swam too far away from Marlin.

3

Marlin met Dory, a fish with short-term memory loss, who agreed to help him.

6

Nemo pretended to be dead, so he was flushed down the toilet and into the ocean.

7

Dory got caught in a net, but Nemo told all the fish to swim down so they could get free.

Character Chart

✏️ **Choose your favorite character and describe them using the words from the personality bank.**

Personality Bank

caring 보살피는	**bold** 용감한	**fearless** 두려움을 모르는
cheerful 쾌활한	**optimistic** 낙관적인	**friendly** 다정한
curious 호기심이 많은	**heroic** 영웅적인	**active** 활동적인
chatty 수다스러운	**careful** 조심하는	**protective** 보호하려고 하는

Stick Here!

My favorite character is

_____ .

I think _____ is

_____ ,

_____ ,

and _____ .

* There is an example answer for you to refer to on page 63.

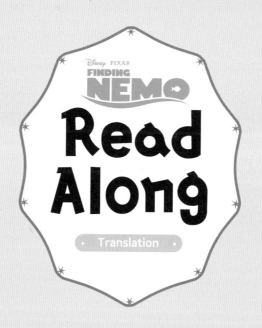

Disney · PIXAR
FINDING NEMO

Read Along

Translation

p.2

❊ 니모는 자신의 아빠인, 말린과 함께, 그레이트 베리어 리프에서 조용한 삶을 살고 있는 작은 흰동가리 물고기였습니다. 니모는 모험을 동경했지만, 말린은 바다의 위험들을 걱정했습니다. 그는 니모가 자신의 시야에서 벗어나는 것을 거의 허락하지 않았습니다.

p.3

❊ 입학 첫날, 말린은 니모와 그의 새로운 친구들이 가파른 절벽 너머로 헤엄쳐 가 보라고 서로를 부추기는 소리를 우연히 들었습니다.

"자, 니모! 너는 얼마나 멀리까지 갈 수 있어?"

p.4

❊ 말린은 당황해서 어쩔 줄 몰랐습니다. "니모, 너는 네가 헤엄을 잘 치지 못한다는 걸 알잖니."

"저 헤엄 잘 칠 수 있어요, 아빠. 알겠어요?"

p.5

❊ 니모는 수면에 떠 있는 보트를 향해 쏜살같이 헤엄쳐 올라갔습니다. 그의 아빠는 그의 뒤에서 소리쳤어요. "여기로 돌아와! 아빠가 말했지, 여기로 돌아오라고, 당장!"

니모가 헤엄치고 있을 때, 그의 뒤에서 한 잠수부가 나타났습니다.

p.6

❊ 잠수부는 그물망을 꺼내고 니모를 잡았습니다. 그러고 나서 그는 자신의 보트로 돌아가서 속도를 내며 가 버렸는데, 그때 실수로 자신의 잠수용 마스크 중 하나를 쳐서 보트 밖으로 떨어뜨렸습니다.

p.7

❊ 말린은 보트를 쫓아갔지만, 그것은 너무 빨랐어요. "니모! 니모, 안 돼! **안 돼!**" 말린은 사방으로 찾아 헤맸습니다. "누구 보트를 본 적 있어? 네?"

p.8

✳ 말린은 곧 도움을 주겠다고 제안한 도리라는 이름의 블루탱 물고기와 마주쳤습니다.

"이봐, 내가 보트를 봤어! 그리고 보트는 이쪽으로 갔어! 나를 따라와!"

말린이 따라가자, 도리는 홱 돌아보았어요. "나를 그만 좀 따라와, 알겠어?"

"너 무슨 소리를 하는 거야? 너는 보트가 어느 쪽으로 갔는지 나에게 알려 주는 중이잖아."

---

p.9

✳ 도리는 놀란 듯 보였고, 그러더니 슬프게 고개를 가로저었습니다. "정말 미안해. 사실, 나-나는 단기 기억 상실증을 앓고 있거든."

도리가 자신을 도울 수 없다는 것을 깨닫고, 말린은 떠나려고 몸을 돌렸다가 자신이 상어와 마주 보고 있다는 것을 깨달았습니다!

---

p.10

✳ 상어는 도리와 말린을 오래전에 침몰한 보트에서 열리는 "모임"에 초대했습니다.

도리는 신이 났어요. "파티 같은 걸 말하는 거야?"

보트 안에는 두 마리의 다른 상어들이 있었고, 그들은 다 같이 맹세했습니다: "나는 착한 상어다, 생각 없이 먹어 치우는 기계가 아니다. 물고기는 친구이지, 음식이 아니다."

그들이 말을 하는 사이, 말린은 올려다보았고 잠수부의 마스크를 보았어요! 도리는 끈에 무언가 쓰여 있다는 것을 알아차렸습니다. 그것은 그들이 니모를 찾는 것을 도와줄 단서가 될지도 몰랐어요! 말린과 도리는 마스크를 가지고, 서둘러 "파티"를 떠났습니다.

---

p.13

✳ 수 마일 떨어진 곳에서, 니모는 어느 치과 의사의 진료실에 있는 수조로 옮겨져 있었습니다. 그곳에는 한 무리의 엉뚱한 열대어들이 살고 있었어요. 그 물고기들과 펠리컨인, 그들의 친구 나이젤은, 치과 의사가 일하는 것을 구경하며 시간을 보냈습니다.

p.14

✹ 그날 밤, 니모는 자신이 치과 의사의 조카인, 달라에게 선물로 건네질 것이라는 사실을 알게 되었습니다. 수조의 물고기 무리는 그에게 달라의 물고기들이 절대 오래 살지 못한다고 경고했습니다. 니모의 새로운 친구들은 그에게 어떤 나쁜 일이 생기는 것을 원하지 않았어요.

그들의 대장인, 길이, 지휘를 맡았습니다. "우리는 그가 탈출하도록 도울 거야."

길은 만약 누군가가 수조의 물 필터를 고장나게 할 수 있다면, 치과 의사가 수족관을 청소하기 위해 물고기들을 수조 밖으로 꺼낼 것이라고 설명했습니다. 그가 물고기들을 비닐봉지에 담으면, 그들은 창밖으로 굴러 나가 항구로 뛰어들어 탈출할 수 있었어요.

하지만 누가 그 위험한 필터를 고장 낼 만큼 용감하겠어요?

---

p.16

✹ 바다 깊은 곳에서, 도리와 말린은 캄캄한 협곡에 다다랐습니다.

말린은 도리가 마스크에 쓰여 있는 것을 읽을 수 있도록 무시무시한 아귀의 빛나는 더듬이를 꼭 잡고 있으려고 버둥거렸어요. "P. 셔먼, 월라비 가 42번지, 시드니."

---

p.17

✹ 갑자기, 아귀가 풀려났습니다. "피해!" 그 거대한 물고기는 그들의 위로 돌진하다가, 마스크와 바위 사이에 몸이 끼어 버렸어요. 말린은 안도의 한숨을 내쉬었습니다. 이것은 엄청난 모험이 되어 가고 있었습니다!

---

p.19

✹ 말린과 도리는 시드니로 향했습니다. 갑자기, 도리는 조그마한 해파리와 마주쳤습니다. "나는 이 아이를 스퀴시라고 부를래, 그리고 이 아이는 내 거야."

하지만 스퀴시는 혼자가 아니었어요. 곧, 그들은 치명적인 해파리들의 숲으로 온통 둘러싸였습니다. 해파리들은 도리를, 그리고 말린도 쏘았고, 그들을 힘 없고 피곤하게 느끼도록 만들었습니다.

바다가 그의 주변에서 점점 희미해져 갈 때, 말린이 마지막으로 본 것은 거대한 바다거북의 그림자였습니다.

p.20

✻ 말린이 깨어났을 때, 그는 바다거북의 등껍질 위에 있었습니다. 바다거북은 자신을 소개했어요. "친구! 내 이름은 크러시야."

그들 주위에는, 수백 마리의 바다거북들이 번개처럼 빠른 해류를 타고 이동하고 있었습니다. 말린은 크러시와 그의 아들 스쿼트에게 자신이 니모를 찾아 나선 이야기를 들려주었습니다. "나는 여기에서 아주, 아주 먼 어떤 산호초에서 살고 있는데...."

p.21

✻ 도리는 이미 그 이야기를 잊은 채였습니다. "이 이야기는 재미있을 거야. 나는 알 수 있어!"

스쿼트는 이 이야기를 바닷가재에게 말했고, 바닷가재는 돌고래에게 말했고, 곧 이 이야기는 멀리 시드니까지 퍼져나가, 그곳에서 펠리컨 나이젤이 그 소식을 들었습니다.

p.22

✻ 나이젤은 니모에게 알리기 위해 치과 진료실로 재빨리 날아갔습니다. "네 아빠가 너를 찾으려고 온 바다와 맞서 싸우고 있어. 그리고 들리는 말에 의하면, 그는 바로 지금 이곳으로 오고 있대—시드니로 말이야!"

"정말이야?" 니모는 자신의 아빠가 그렇게 모험심이 강하다는 것을 믿을 수 없었어요! 말린은 그를 구하기 위해 모든 위험을 무릅쓰고 있었습니다. 니모는 자신이 언젠가 집에 돌아갈 것이라면, 자신 또한, 용감해져야 한다는 것을 깨달았습니다.

p.23

✻ 그는 깊은 숨을 들이마시고 조심스럽게 수조의 필터에 조약돌 하나를 끼워 넣어, 빙빙 돌아가는 필터의 날개들을 멈추게 했습니다. 곧, 수조가 아주 더러워져서 치과 의사는 그곳을 청소해야만 할 것입니다....

p.24

✻ 하지만 아침에도, 수조는 여전히 깨끗했습니다! 필터가 밤사이에 교체되어서, 그들의 탈출 계획을 망쳐 버리고 말았어요. 그때, 치과 의사가 물속으로 그물망을 집어넣어, 니모를 잡았습니다.

"도와줘요!"

재빨리 생각하며, 길은 그물망 안으로 뛰어들어 니모에게 소리쳤습니다. "아래로 헤엄쳐!" 그는 그렇게 했고, 그물망을 아래로 끌어내려 거기에서 탈출했지만—치과 의사가 들고 있던 비닐봉지 안으로 곧장 들어가고 말았어요.

p.25

✻ 치과 의사는 달라에게 그 봉지를 건넸지만, 그때 그는 배를 위로 드러낸, 봉지 안의 니모를 보았습니다. 니모는 자신의 친구들에게 윙크했습니다. 그는 죽은 척을 하고 있을 뿐이었어요. 물고기 무리는 환호했습니다. "그는 변기로 흘려보내질 거야. 그는 여기에서 나가게 될 거라고!"

p.26

✻ 시드니 외곽에서, 말린과 도리는 나이젤을 만났고, 나이젤은 곧장 그들을 데리고 치과 진료실로 날아갔습니다. 펠리컨은 그 두 물고기를 자신의 부리 안에 태운 채 진료실 안으로 날아왔어요.

p.27

✻ 말린은 니모가 봉지 안에서 뒤집힌 채 떠 있는 것을 보았어요. "니모!" 말린은 자신의 아들이 죽었다고 생각했습니다.

치과 의사는 나이젤을 밖으로 쫓아냈습니다. "밖으로 나가. 그리고 밖에 있으라고!"

p.28

✻ 나이젤은 항구로 돌아갔습니다. 그는 말린과 도리를 물속에 떨어뜨려 주었습니다. 말린은 도리를 남겨 둔 채, 바다로 헤엄쳐 갔어요. "우리는 너무 늦었어. 나는 이제 집에 갈 거야."

p.29

✳ 말린이 떠난 후, 니모가 근처의 배수관에서 헤엄쳐 나왔습니다. 그는 변기 물에 흘려보내진 것이었어요! 니모는 제자리에서 원을 그리며 헤엄치고 있는 도리를 발견했습니다. "괜찮으세요? 저는 니모예요."

"아아! 네가 니모구나!" 도리는 기뻐하며 그를 껴안았습니다.

---

p.30

✳ 니모와 도리는 말린을 찾아보았고, 근처에 있는 어장에서 그를 발견했습니다.

"아빠!"

"니모! 아빠가 갈게, 니모!"

그들이 서로를 향해 헤엄쳐 갈 때, 커다란 그물이 물속으로 떨어져 많은 물고기를 잡았고, 그중에는 도리도 있었어요! 하지만 니모는 정확히 무엇을 해야 할지 알고 있었습니다. "모든 물고기들에게 아래로 헤엄치라고 말해 주세요!"

---

p.31

✳ 니모는 돕기 위해 심지어 그물 안으로 헤엄쳐 들어가기도 했습니다. 다 함께, 물고기들은 그물이 찢어질 때까지 아래로 헤엄쳤습니다. 모두가 풀려났어요!

---

p.32

✳ 몇 주 후, 니모는 집으로 돌아왔고 학교에 갈 준비가 되어 있었습니다. 이번에는, 말린도, 준비가 되어 있었어요. 그는 자신의 아들이 스스로를 돌볼 수 있다는 것을 알고 있었습니다.

니모는 헤엄쳐 가면서 지느러미를 흔들어 인사했습니다. "다녀올게요, 아빠. 아, 잠깐만요! 저 깜빡한 게 있어요!" 그는 되돌아 헤엄쳐 가서 말린을 안아 주었습니다. "사랑해요, 아빠."

말린은 미소를 지었습니다. "나도, 너를 사랑한단다, 아들아. 이제, 가서 모험을 하렴!"

Part 1   p.14 – 17

Vocabulary Quiz

1

O	H	A	D	R	K	A	I	D	L	K	L
B	W	L	M	R	S	D	J	Y	I	N	Z
A	D	V	E	N	T	U	R	E	V	O	M
R	Y	S	D	T	G	U	I	O	S	C	V
E	X	T	Z	G	D	R	H	I	O	K	I
L	P	D	A	N	G	E	R	G	F	H	S
Y	Z	N	E	M	O	T	S	F	G	W	I
S	D	O	R	Y	I	U	H	A	R	B	G
C	R	F	I	G	U	R	E	R	E	A	H
Q	D	H	T	D	T	N	K	Y	E	F	T
K	I	T	A	P	D	L	N	G	F	R	M
F	C	H	A	S	E	Y	D	I	Z	X	Z

reef 암초 / **adventure** 모험 /
danger 위험 / **barely** 거의 ~ 아니게 /
sight 시야 / **return** 돌아가다 /
knock 쳐서 움직이게 하다 /
chase 뒤쫓다 / **figure** 판단하다

2   1 surface   2 steep   3 dart
4 clownfish   5 diver   6 toward
7 blue tang   8 search   9 mask
10 overboard   11 bump into
12 appear   13 face-to-face

ANSWER
He searched everywhere and
asked if anybody had seen a boat.

Comprehension Quiz

1   2 - 1 - 4 - 3

2   1 b   2 b   3 c

3   1 false   2 true   3 false
4 false   5 true

Part 2   p.24 – 27

Vocabulary Quiz

1

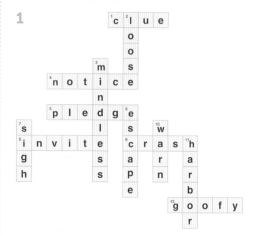

2   1 wedge   2 antenna   3 niece
4 tank   5 pelican   6 canyon
7 get-together   8 filter   9 gang
10 struggle   11 anglerfish   12 strap
13 tropical fish   14 dentist

ANSWER
They did not want anything bad to
happen to him.

Comprehension Quiz

1   1 c   2 a

2   1 c   2 b   3 a

3   1 true   2 false   3 false
4 false   5 true

Vocabulary Quiz

1

M	Q	F	B	P	X	E	A	F	E	P	A
A	U	O	I	D	I	I	F	L	O	W	L
C	U	R	R	E	N	T	E	R	Y	P	O
M	R	G	A	E	T	L	G	I	L	F	N
C	Y	E	B	A	R	A	K	F	A	D	E
O	A	T	O	Z	O	L	S	H	A	R	K
D	T	K	L	M	D	A	I	U	D	S	B
E	L	E	A	P	U	L	E	F	K	P	D
A	V	A	T	O	C	A	L	Q	J	R	H
D	Q	Z	K	L	E	N	T	I	R	E	T
L	B	I	H	E	Q	N	A	E	I	A	S
Y	K	E	S	H	A	D	O	W	N	D	E

alone 혼자 / **entire** 전체의 /
deadly 치명적인 / **fade** 점점 희미해지다 /
shadow 그림자 / **introduce** 소개하다 /
current 해류 / **forget** 잊다 /
spread 퍼지다

2 1 pebble   2 surround
    3 sea turtle   4 swirl   5 blade
    6 shell   7 forest   8 shadow
    9 weak   10 sting   11 jellyfish
    12 teeny-tiny   13 jam

ANSWER

The pelican told him that Marlin was searching the entire ocean looking for him.

Comprehension Quiz

1   1 - 4 - 3 - 2

2   1 b   2 a   3 a

3   1 false   2 true   3 true
     4 true   5 true

Vocabulary Quiz

1

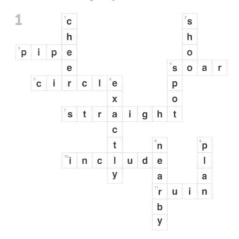

2 1 upside down   2 slip   3 pretend
    4 capture   5 flush   6 include
    7 plastic bag   8 hand   9 belly
    10 wave   11 charge   12 wink

ANSWER

The pelican went inside with the two fish in his beak.

Comprehension Quiz

1   1 c   2 c

2   1 c   2 a   3 b

3   1 false   2 true   3 false
     4 true   5 true

Character Chart   p.54

EXAMPLE

My favorite character is Dory.
I think Dory(she) is cheerful, optimistic, and chatty.

Read-Along

초판 발행   2023년 6월 21일

지은이   Disney Press
번역   문정화 명채린
콘텐츠제작   정소이 홍하늘 Julie Tofflemire
영문감수   Sherwood Choe
편집   강지희 박새미
디자인   박새롬 이순영
저작권   김보경
마케팅   김보미 정경훈

기획   김승규
펴낸이   이수영
펴낸곳   롱테일북스
출판등록   제2015-000191호
주소   04033 서울특별시 마포구 양화로 113(서교동), 3층
전자메일   help@ltinc.net

ISBN 979-11-91343-57-1 14740

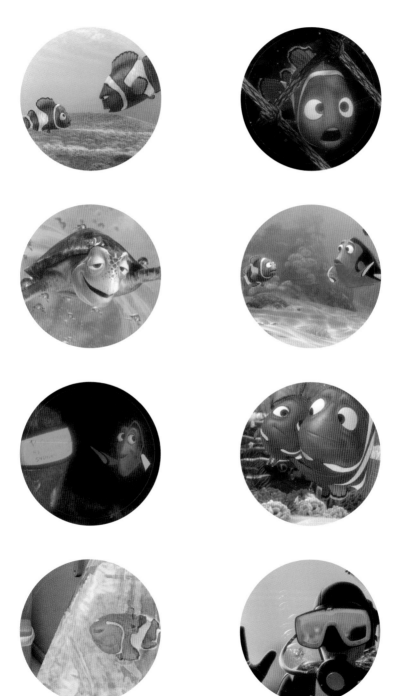

NEMO

MARLIN

DORY

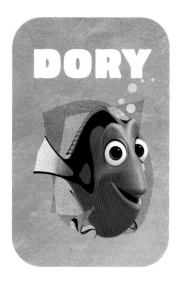

NIGEL

GILL

CRUSH